*An
Angel
in the
Works*

for Bill Latta
fellow poet on
the occasion of
the Ride Off any Hannyon
Reading
April /84

Donated to
Augustana University College
by

William C. Latta

An Angel in the Works

ROBERT HILLES

oolichan books

LANTZVILLE, BRITISH COLUMBIA

1983

Canadian Cataloguing in Publication Data

Hilles, Robert.
    An angel in the works

Poems.
ISBN 0-88982-052-X

I. Title.
PS8565.144A84 1983   C811'.54   C83-091478-1
PR9199.3.H54A84 1983

Publication of this book has been financially
assisted by the Canada Council.

Published by
OOLICHAN BOOKS
P.O. Box 10, Lantzville, B.C. VOR 2HO

Printed in Canada by
MORRISS PRINTING COMPANY LTD.
Victoria, British Columbia, Canada

For Becky

Acknowledgements

Some of these poems have appeared or will appear in the following magazines:

event, The Fiddlehead, Prism international, NeWest Review, Writ, Northern Light, Waves, Island, and *The Camrose Review.*

The author also wishes to thank the Alberta Cultural Fund and the Canada Council for grants received during the writing of this book.

Contents

Part Three: *The Black and White Word*

Part One
This Sudden Emotion

THE YOU AND I OF LOVE

1

i say to you
i have loved only the shape
of what we are
only the renewal that
we are a part of but
escape without
i follow the imagination
only as long as i know
i can find my way back
every vision is contained
by a larger one
every conversation ends with another
you and i know that the magic
is in the moment of discovery
when the emotions are sudden
when lovers find each other
for the first time

2

my mother hides herself
away from view
i call to her
the names of my children
and my children's children
she tells me that
women are soft and must not
deny their husbands their pleasure
she lives in a basement as
small and dark as death
she sobs as i close 100 doors
i know that the darkness is only in eyes
her face is aging with each new word uttered
i want to give her my exact address
but she is already mailing birthday cards
to my children
i want to hold her hands
and cry for all the things she
was not able to do as a woman

3

i want to tell you about my father
a man with small hands and eyes
that hide behind glasses
he worked harder than he needed
and showed me how the movement
of hands control the eye
his face recedes into itself
avoiding the daylight
his clothes always need repair
the contact when we part
is so brief and unsure
through him you and i touch
as lovers we can only kiss
from our imagined selves
you only let me find you
in the dark so that your body
remains mysterious
the smells are more real than the touching
you sing in my ear
the tremble so delicate
i struggle to say things
that are the most perfect
i must or everything slips
through my grip and breaks in the air
breaks in front of my helpless eyes

THESE OLD HANDS I SPEAK WITH

even the most beautiful song
can not save the voice
we are caught inside
the very sound we breathe
the throat is a graceful prison

our mouths are soft and moist
when they meet and for a moment
we are free from our old awkwardness
and forget all that is impossible
between us

these old hands
have their own intelligence as
they slide across your body
i could never make words do that

KINGS OF THE WILD FRONTIER

there is no notation but in death
we speak across the frontiers of knowledge
your anger so much larger
than the world
my voice an old man
singing of new rehearsals with death
we are alive but
only inside of heads

i list the names of everything
i am convinced exists
there is a ballet that moves
behind and in front of the words
let us not compare things
but make lists to refresh our memories

we quarrel from different worlds
and have long names for our despair
we rent rooms to die in
and toast conflicting versions of
the same story
each story is told over and over
but is only told once
each new voice
returns to the beginning

15

i love the way
your hair lies
free on your head
you are so soft
i know only one half of a memory
i am inside the world
that is inside me
i find your hand in mine
it's not an argument
it doesn't explain how we belong
inside this room together
listening to jazz

my hand in yours
we share that
nothing is explained
we hint at each other
we know the real
but love the dream

THIS IS HOW LOVELY WE ARE

at night we run through
fields of wheat the stalks
banging against our legs
we run farther and farther away
from any place we have ever been

our love is not alone
it expands beyond us
growing larger and harder to bear
sometimes at night sleeping together
our body heat makes us both sweat
we find new languages
to speak with and discover
new places to move to
we dance on our backs and sides
and are as primitive as land
and as new as each breath

each morning we find new
things to eat by opening
the door of the refrigerator
the room turns over and over
changing size and shape

the words laid aside
we move with our heads clear
we fall upon each other
and touch always so softly softly
in the beginning
we know no songs
our voices have withered
the skins on our bodies
hide less and less of the bones they cover

we long to love now
alone in this room
our names and sounds gone
our touch is salty and dry
this is how lovely we can be
this is how lovely we are

LOVING YOU

when i hold you
i know there will be minutes,
days, months when it will
not be like this
as we move apart
the motion is like breathing

when i say i love you
i know there are times when i forget
the details of this room
the color of your hair
the warmth of your cheek
the kind of man i dreamed i would be

tonight we light candles
and talk of many things
but i will only remember
the shadow of your hand on my cheek
and your thighs so real
my hand hestitates
before it moves towards them

EVEN AS YOU SPEAK SOMEONE IS DYING

i said to her that i was in love
by the side of the road

i was out on the prairie looking for a real
crocus
i was out on the prairie not for a moment but
forever
there was a pickup truck leaving a trail of
dust
there were some flowers without
names
i was waiting for something that had already
happened
when i turned the sunlight turned with
me
spraying the fields with its
heat

the need to know makes you
self conscious
and even as you speak someone is dying

but death is not a scarecrow or a crow
or a flat prairie landscape or that crocus
i didn't find

it's the return from voice

THESE NOTES I TAKE ARE MEANT
TO DESCRIBE

the dream is in the arm in
the finger
in the movement of numb objects

you worship the poison you
just swallowed
the pain in your lungs is
a reminder that life is only
suspended on air
the balance of the dream
the maddening lonely gesture
of the death song

your surroundings are plain
the height above sea level is marginal
any setting can be a
theatre for death
any surrounding can be
a landscape for love

i know you are trapped in your own
master plan and have left the world
permanently
today we watch each other
from the distance of words
had we not acted like this
perhaps the whole world
would have happened a different way

TONIGHT ON THIS TRAIN

you are silent too
the voices that we rehearse
abandon us like nervous ghosts
we could be here a long time
waiting to undress the lovers inside us

tonight the world reveals
a new angle from a familiar distance
i look out the train window
searching for lights
i know the distance is there
the lights merely remain lights
this night the world is
made new with shadows
the movements reconstruct memories

and on this train alone
i know how much i miss you
i discover your hands caressing me
i can hear your voice in my ear
the love song it forms
changes this motion through night
into the dance of breath

LANDSCAPES

your movements are small
every room seems
just a little too large
and at the window
following your steps
the sky and clouds
invade as if the landscape
was no longer
separate from the eyes

everything else is
a gift
the memory escaping despair
and when i find
your arms at night
there is no landscape
except the closing
of two hearts together

HANDS

we spend all our lives
warming hands blowing
onto them slapping them
on our legs
only those who wake
out of dark dreams
reach for their hands first
and then for the light
in such a darkness
there is no history beyond faith

in another country
someone has just said goodbye
to a lover of 15 years
their hands together hold a gospel
you sense that they have
spoken something wild and forbidden
and yet those humble hands
tangled together must never
again be tied behind the back
it's like that too in the morning
i wait for your hand on my penis
those soft strokes make me
want to sing in your ear
and to rest my tongue there
between the notes

Part Two
An Angel in the Works

1

No One Knows Where the Poem Will Go

we will rest awhile
we will participate
later in the dark
our hands over dried faces

the music resounds

the poem descends into the dark
i saw it leave
but was afraid to speak
for fear of being discovered
i only come to things by accident
the rest already reported in other places

when i finally let go only the air
will be forced out of my lungs
until then i
save up for more questions

2

What Do Horses Do At Night

with our knees pressed on hardwood
we know that is not how
the world was invented
we cannot look over our
shoulders and discover a better history
everything we have is expendable
and we are careful now because
it cannot go beyond the moment of belief

only in my arms
are you familiar
i am bothered by many questions
and only by sleeping in different worlds
am i able to get up from your arms
a complete person

3

Deep Structure

there is an echo in every silence

the deep structure is more
than the geological memory
more than remembering the form of air
that your lungs translate
or how your fingers assemble knowledge

how many parts do you have to name
before you discover
that you actually bleed
or feel how your emotions dance free
on the tightrope of your backbone

the blood is always contained
it connects joy with pain
everything separates into itself
but still corresponds to
that larger movement
across the expanding landscape

4

An Improvisation on a Line

"i dreamed last night that your body
had become a gigantic adventure" — JACK SPICER

in that dream
we were speaking a newly discovered
dialect
you were burying the remains of
a casual war
it took you almost all night
later we scrambled to each other's arms
tired but barren to our own speech patterns

i know no words that can
give you a single extra breath

5

This Train Makes No Stops

for us time can get no shorter

all things begin in violence

and the distance that surrounds us
is imagined and real at the same time
you are hanging up the phone
i am passing a hand through my hair
outside a car horn sounds

things move always outwards and inwards
all motion is the exploration of distance
and a hand carving love is as strong
as a hand carving silence

all of us are nomads as if we were
born on highways
our true longing is for the range
and the hills beyond
where only by moving ever onward
does the world really become a place
where we can live

6

Love and Death and All That Jazz

the tribe had breakfast and
no one dreamed of being real

there is no lie or truth only small
dialogues with yourself and others
that is how we live within each other's touch
we are so close to the silence of voice
don't wait for that real thing that is
in your hand
the voice doesn't wait for the words
the song lives in the cords
and dies in the ears

the tribal sound in my throat
doesn't desire microphones or transistors
those nimble fibres shape
only that real pain

7

Correspondence of the Dead

it is only outside the naming
that the objects express themselves
you cannot describe the name
or the proper method of voice
no amount of refusal will
burn old syllables

the name, the poem, the song
do not stop the dying
we speak only in death
and are read only by the dead
the world will die

this shovel i hold
belongs only to the shape of my hand
and not to the name i utter
as it swells in my grip
its shape is important only
to the tension of the act of holding
then as i begin to dig
the motion is as smooth as a dance
and the geometry of the grave
goes unnoticed

words and the night
belong to dead men
people who died nowhere in particular
who spent all their lives
craving their own end
they let their stories occur
wherever they happened

8

An Angel in the Works

this poem is for you jack
for you where the sea crashes without ears
where the sky moves without eyes
in a small room i learn new words
and new ways of speaking

we will collapse without songs
the poem must survive
i know that you were not a big man
you wanted the poem to come on its own
i want to tell you a story
about two lovers alone
in a room
each one is dancing in his own footsteps
they continue to dance
even now as i look in

there is no music nor
need there be
there is an angel in the works
and the lovers are dancing

Part Three
The Black and White Word

WE WILL SURRENDER IN NEW DARK

there are people dying here
that i can't recognize
tiny birds fall out of the sky

we are drawn into the dance
we own so little of what we are
as if the space around us was not
part of our movements

we surrender in new dark
but no one tells the story quite right
the details are changed each time
the throat is moistened

you can see how small death is
how it moves around the room on all fours

the story begins with that image
in birth and death   the secret
is in the transfer
of energy

the message is always held
tightly between the lips
and we want to be primitive
to lay down as ghosts

we are surrounded by light
and survive by
forging our signatures

ALL MY FATHERS HAVE FANTASTIC WOMEN

at daybreak the sun is alone
trying to bury the horizon
there is no voice
no song, no landscape
this is the way
all my fathers have planned it
they become the day
singing in voices primitive and electronic
there has been a death in the family

i slip back behind the house
frightened of the growing light
i feel my throat harden
my hands crumble
there is dried mud on my feet
i can see all my fathers
they have fantastic women
they are standing in a circle
one of them speaks:

> When we leave,
> this ground will poison its children
> the grass will shrivel
> the trees will die
> the air will disappear.

i have no way of dying
i have seen all my fathers
and they have fantastic women
they drift past me like a memory
we have lived together in this small madness
they are prepared to teach me nothing
they are speculating on their own death
all my fathers have fantastic women
that is the magic

ORIGINAL VIOLENCE

For Robin Blaser

under the hot lights
i wait to touch the soft spot
of love

i could have measured
the amount of surprise

the political life of
violence can't be explained by
procedure

when you discuss
the talent of wood
you do not come with fire
or with smoke

you can't sit out in the
open at night
waiting for the dream of language
and then looking at the stars
from that old familiar distance
find the story in the shelter
of a song

i have lived exactly
as instructed

the original violence
names our arrival in time

SOMETHING DOESN'T REST IN THIS PLACE

out the window there is
snow on dark streets
an imposed notion of place
and when i dream the world
always intrudes
when we talk about flesh
and bone and tongue
do we mean something
other than heart and mind

you can list the objects
you live with and how
they separate you from others
but if you touch yourself
when you are dreaming
you will be left there forever

matter drifts around rooms
and finds arms to hold onto
or words to command with
or trees to leap from
or rooms to make love in
and sleeps contained
within soft borders
the tension and power
so delicately hid
late in the night
i get a glass of water
i go from bed to sink
and back again without a light
merely with thirst
and memory to guide me

UPON WAKING I WILL WRITE
THIS DOWN

it's not how small things are
or who the lovers are
the pain is always inside
the particles become smaller and smaller
and yet there is no entrance
no way to get inside

the world is made of mundane things
objects moved around rooms
furniture piled against a wall
the colours trapped in their own name
you can say it, shape it
with your lips but can
never own it

things are shapeless
they fall apart in your hand
you cannot know what
they are or how they feel
even your own body
floats inside of rooms
barely touching the floor
you think you control
the steps but find yourself
at strange destinations
your stomach empty and
your legs mysteriously tired

everything is contrived but real
what i give you is imagined
but pretends to truth
what i say is real
but was learned in dreams

NEW MUSIC

this room
reminds me of you mother
and your soft thighs
on certain nights
our arms are old
and we roll dried leaves
over in our fingers
you expect me someday to
turn into an angel
you instruct me on how
to save the world
i try to get up early each morning
to redecorate it for you

you have grown weary
from giving away your eyes
and you bring me single tears
preserved perfectly in glass
nothing becomes any older
i tell you that we have
a war with history
you are tired of the imagination
we wake up in different countries
each one as fantastic as the other
at night we sleep in awkward positions
we are familiar with the
silent workings of the heart
you remember the language
i was born with
you understand my obsession with hands
when we are tired
there is new music to put on
and new places to remember

SMALL FRUIT

we soon forget the rage
that is never still
even as the vegetation dies
around us and the rivers
turn more and more black
you must suckle small fruit
and charm its sweet nectar
on your tongue
you must eat slowly
let the teeth burn as they chew
the hunger is still there
over and over
only you can feel it inside
the hollow throat

WARM HANDS

with this love
the world dies a little

with these warm hands
i give you an opening
with each touch we discover
there is no gesture complete

you undress slowly for me
i wait for you to fall
into my arms
our bodies have never
been this alive

later i dream
there are people dying
outside the window
the world somehow belonging
to those falling corpses
as we love together
everything else transforms into death

outside the world
of lovers everything
continues to get smaller and die
there are refugees whose
words i will never understand
they must be fed
is that what we mean
when we say that lovers
must fall to find
the platform of the world

many have died
from the want of love
we know there is pain
but is it greater than the unnoticed
death in the silence of a drying place

I REMEMBER SOME THINGS CLEARLY

there are flies in vacant lots
their tiny blue bodies sparkling

vultures sing on rooftops
their beaks twisted like orange saxaphones
syrup notes cling to the windows
they are peaceful birds
their wings kiss the air
ever so softly like
a late night evangelist
on the radio whose voice
draws your thoughts first in
one direction and then in another

worms are miracle workers
but they are always mistaken
for death itself

i feel i must apologize
to these things that live
cast so long in one role
i will open the doors of this poem
and let them go free

THAT MORNING

i could say that
it's raining outside
that starving children
are getting wet
that innocent people are
being hung in the rain
i could cut off my right hand
and send it to you wrapped in brown paper

it's too easy to remember
all of your own pain
it's too easy to die alone
pretending to follow some
badly worded creed
i want to reach out
to find the stomach of things
i want to explain the maps
that are buried in primitive gardens
i want to tell stories that
erupt from the throat
i want the world not to
collapse but to lift up
to look away from the fires

but there will be mornings
too when the world will arise
alone forgotten hiding in cities
there will be days when people
will die swiftly
the air still warm in their throats
there will be months when lovers
will not find each other
but the tragedy is in failing
to look the way of the turning sun

in the morning we can
awake alone in our soft embrace
we can turn our sparkling bodies over
we can be heroes just for one day

I LIVE IN SILENCE

when things don't fit
we arrange the lines
as we need them

we are tired of
undressing in small rooms
where the light is too bright
and the smell is as primitive as skin

i stand at the window
and as i move it follows me
loosening the edges of the world
i breath the sounds
that i am singing
over and over
the song changes only as i find
the inside of my throat tightening

THE BLACK AND WHITE WORD

you must read this
by holding it up to a mirror

look at the mirror again
and you will see in your eyes
the lack of sleep
the baby and the old man
both instantly there

the world is behind the wall
behind the mirror
each part placed perfectly next
to the other the shape
comes apart in your hands

WHEN YOU DIE

across the road
there is a garden
and when you die
the dust you inhabit
will be spread over that ground
so thinly it will never
again hold an image

when you are home at night
with the windows closed
and the heat turned down
do you bring small flowers to your lips
while the light crawls into the room
as if from a darker world

the soft blood
rests in old veins
i reach around you
to protect an impression
i once had
i tell you of my father
how he still holds me
in his hands
and how he washes flowers until
they shed their pale colours

we feel we have survived
all kinds of small horrors
you turn your face
in this special light
we stand up together
and reach for our separate clothes
as our eyes disappear out a window
we long for rain
to make the escape more real

we long to hold something
important in our hands
and for each heart to be
capable of more than just beating
alone in its prison of ribs